love,
Cadhla

500 *Quotes*
on Love and Kindness
in a Lined Journal

Cadhla Logan

MAD MOUNTAIN
PUBLISHING

*includes
black-and-white
illustrations,
100+ pages
for notes,
plus
Gran's
favourite
quotes!!*

ISBN 978 0 578 36078 2

Credits

Front Cover Art
Courtesy of Willgard Krause

Illustrations
 "love" Natality © fotosearch.ie
 "phoenix" Derriva © fotosearch.ie
 "kindness" dip © fotosearch.ie
 "circle of life" Transia © fotosearch.ie
 "life" puhimec © fotosearch.ie
 "loss" krisina0702 © fotosearch.ie
 "the sea" Jesser © fotosearch.ie
 "memories" jstan © fotosearch.ie
 "dreams" sliplee © fotosearch.ie
 "hope" puhimec © fotosearch.ie
 "Celtic buckle and bells" rocich © fotosearch.ie
 "Triquetra Trinity Knot" courtesy Wikimedia Commons
 "Eire map" Schwanbenblitz © fotosearch.ie
 "The Dragon" Vyusur © fotosearch.ie
Other Photos courtesy Adobe and Pixabay

Cover and Interior Design
Cadhla Logan, Dublin, Ireland

**MAD MOUNTAIN
PUBLISHING**

*For*_____

_____

❧

MO GHRÁ THU
MO STÓR...

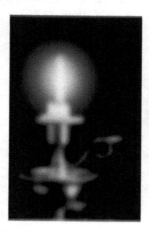

*"I think perhaps I will
always hold a candle
for you — even until it
burns my hand. And
when the light has
long since gone ....
I will be there in the
darkness holding what
remains, quite simply
because I cannot let go."*
— Ranata Suzuki

With enormous thanks and
eternal gratitude to
Willgard Krause,
for graciously allowing their
incomparable fantasy art
for my book cover!

CONTENTS

♡

Like many children, I grew up within a difficult family.
I tried everything to escape, physically and mentally.
I remember thinking I must have the worst pain in the
world to bear, trapped amongst these people with their
quarrels, fights, accusations, hatred. Abuse seemed to
know no end, my physical scars still visible on my face
even today.

But there were good days, those when I escaped into my
books. How I loved moments of peace and life within
those fantasy worlds and long-past times, how I wanted
to be left there, far from the turmoil I could do nothing
to make better, much less to end. The local library and
a bookshop inside an elderly lady's cottage, became
my favourite haunts, my sanctuaries.

I loved reading but I found it difficult to concentrate.
Memorizing was almost impossible, but I started writing
things down to read over again later... and this is how I
came to love and collect quotations. A handful of words,
like a magical faery dust, would instantly transport
me back to my happy childhood escapes.

The quotes within are some my life-long favourites, and
Gran shares a few of hers with you. You will see several
by the same authors, also, please note, we decided
to not create an artificial length to each section. There is a
randomness that reflects that of our own lives, having little
time for reading, we always feel so grateful to find a few
moments to spend with a book.

This book is not meant to be read straight-through, but over days,
weeks, months. We hope you enjoy our collection and, too, that these
words perhaps will speak to someone and give them the comfort they
seek and that they once gave me. It is never too late to craft yourself
a safe and happy future...you just have to find the words to inspire the
motivation you need. :>

love,
Cadhla, Gran, and Mix

love

love

"You can't give your heart to a wild thing."
— *Truman Capote*

*"And it was a most remarkable, a most
moving glance, as if for a moment,
a lighthouse had looked at me."*
— *Ford Madox Ford*

*"I have spread my dreams under your feet.
Tread softly because you tread on my dreams."*
— *William Butler Yeats*

*"To fall in love is to create a religion
that has a fallible god."*
— *Jorge Luis Borges*

*"I know I am but summer to your heart, and not
the full four seasons of the year."*
— *Edna St. Vincent Millay*

*"Trust your heart if the seas catch fire,
live by love though the stars walk backward."*
— *e.e. cummings*

*"His eyes were the same colour as the sea
in a postcard someone sends you when
they love you, but not enough to stay."*
— Warsan Shire

*"Let love be the gravestone
Lying on my life."*
— Anna Akhmatova

*"I would like to be the air that inhabits you
for a moment only. I would like to be that unnoticed
and that necessary."*
— Margaret Atwood

*"For he would be thinking of love
Till the stars had run away
And the shadows eaten the moon."*
— William Butler Yeats

*"The day the power of love overrules
the love of power, the world will know peace."*
— Mahatma Gandhi

*"Love is that condition in which the happiness
of another person is essential to your own."*
— Robert A. Heinlein

"We shall be everything to each other.
Nothing else shall be of any consequence."
— *Kate Chopin*

"He loved her, he loved her, and until he'd loved her
she had never minded being alone...."
— *Truman Capote*

"You are my sun, my moon, and all my stars."
— *e.e. cummings*

"It is love, not reason, that is stronger than death."
— *Thomas Mann*

"I would have followed you to hell and back...
if only you'd lead me back."
— *Ranata Suzuki*

"Your voice is wild and simple.
You are untranslatable
Into any one tongue."
— *Anna Akhmatova*

"The heart of a mother is a deep abyss at the bottom
of which you will always find forgiveness."
— *Honoré de Balzac*

*"Ah, lips that say one thing, while the heart
thinks another."*
— Alexandre Dumas

"You are my peace, my solace, my salvation."
— Jean-Baptiste Poquelin, Molière

*"A woman knows the face of the man
she loves like a sailor knows the open sea."*
— Honoré de Balzac

*"I envy everyone secretly,
I secretly love everything."*
— Osip Mandelstam

*"Nobody has ever measured, not even poets,
how much the heart can hold."*
— Zelda Fitzgerald

*"Sometimes you have to get to know someone
really well to realize you're really strangers."*
— Mary Richards

*"Though lovers be lost, love shall not;
And death shall have no dominion."*
— Dylan Thomas

"What greater gift than the love of a cat."
— *Charles Dickens*

*"To love or have loved, that is enough. Ask nothing
further. There is no other pearl to be found
in the dark folds of life."*
— *Victor Hugo*

*"The possession of knowledge does not kill the sense of
wonder and mystery. There is always more mystery."*
— *Anaïs Nin*

*"We are like islands in the sea,
separate on the surface but connected in the deep."*
— *William James*

*"Give me your hand out of the depths
sown by your sorrows."*
— *Pablo Neruda*

*"He was now in that state of fire that she loved.
She wanted to be burnt."*
— *Anaïs Nin*

"When love arrives, all needs and flaws are gone."
— *Yunus Emre*

"I'll risk everything together with you."
— *Henrik Ibsen*

"Love is space and time measured by the heart."
— *Marcel Proust*

"I want nothing from love, in short, but love."
— *Sidonie Gabrielle Colette*

*"You don't find love, it finds you.
It's got a little bit to do with destiny, fate,
and what's written in the stars."*
— *Anaïs Nin*

*"To feel the love of people whom we love
is a fire that feeds our life."*
— *Pablo Neruda*

"A loving heart is the truest wisdom."
— *Charles Dickens*

"The more one judges, the less one loves."
— *Honoré de Balzac*

"Only love, and not reason, yields kind thoughts."
— *Thomas Mann*

"We shall be everything to each other.
Nothing else shall be of any consequence."
— *Kate Chopin*

"Love is hard to find, hard to keep, and hard to forget."
— *Alysha Speer*

"Love is an endless mystery because there is no
reasonable cause that could explain it."
— *Rabindranath Tagore*

"The truth is simple; you do not die from love.
You only wish you did."
— *Erica Jong*

"The words 'I Love You' kill, and resurrect millions,
in less than a second."
— *Aberjhani*

"If people can just love each other a little bit,
they can be so happy."
— *Émile Zola*

"Women are meant to be loved, not understood."
— *Oscar Wilde*

"No one worth possessing can quite be possessed."
— Sara Teasdale

"Everything is moved by love."
— Osip Mandelstam

"Love is wiser than wisdom."
— Umberto Eco

"Love is a striking example of how little reality means to us."
— Marcel Proust

"He was both everything I could ever want... And nothing I could ever have..."
— Ranata Suzuki

"We were together. I forget the rest."
— Walt Whitman

"If the human heart sometimes finds moments of pause as it ascends the slopes of affection, it rarely halts on the way down."
— Honoré de Balzac

*"But hurry, let's entwine ourselves as one,
our mouth broken, our soul bitten by love,
as time discovers us safely destroyed."*
— *Federico Garcia Lorca*

*"You are always new. The last of your kisses
was ever the sweetest, the last smile the
brightest, the last movement
the gracefullest."*
— *John Keats*

"Though lovers be lost love shall not."
— *Dylan Thomas*

*"I see you everywhere, in the stars, in the river,
to me you're everything that exists;
the reality of everything."*
— *Virginia Woolf*

*"But I love your feet only because they walked
upon the earth and upon the wind
and upon the waters until they found me."*
— *Pablo Neruda*

*"It was love at first sight, at last sight,
at ever and ever sight."*
— *Vladimir Nabokov*

"What you remember saves you."
— *W. S. Merwin*

kindness

kindness

*"Kindness is a language which the deaf can hear
and the blind can see."*
— Mark Twain

*"Be kind, for everyone you meet is
fighting a harder battle."*
— Plato

*"You cannot do a kindness too soon,
for you never know how soon it will be too late."*
— Ralph Waldo Emerson

"Never lose a chance of saying a kind word."
— William Makepeace Thackeray

*"Moments of kindness and reconciliation
are worth having, even if the parting
has to come sooner or later."*
— Alice Munro

"Be kind. Always if you have a choice, be kind."
— Anne Rice

*"Because I haven't yet learned the simplest
and most important thing of all: the world is difficult,
and we are all breakable. So just be kind."*
— *Caitlin Moran*

*"We reveal most about ourselves
when we speak about others."*
— *Kamand Kojouri*

*"Today I bent the truth to be kind,
and I have no regret, for I am far surer
of what is kind than I am of what is true."*
— *Robert Brault*

*"The simplest acts of kindness are by far
more powerful than a thousand heads
bowing in prayer."*
— *Mahatma Gandhi*

*"No act of kindness, no matter how small,
is ever wasted."*
— *Aesop*

*"What I want is so simple I almost can't say it:
elementary kindness."*
— *Barbara Kingsolver*

"A kind gesture can reach a wound
that only compassion can heal."
— Steve Maraboli

"Tenderness and kindness are not signs of weakness
and despair, but manifestations of strength
and resolution."
— Kahlil Gibran

"There is nothing so rewarding as to make people
realize that they are worthwhile in this world."
— Bob Anderson

"Look to be treated by others
as you have treated others."
— Publilius Syrus

"Three things in human life are important:
the first is to be kind; the second is to be kind;
and the third is to be kind."
— Henry James

"All values in this world are, more or less,
questionable, but the most important thing
in life is human kindness."
— Yevgeny Yevtushenko

"Come live in my heart and pay no rent."
— *Samuel Lover*

friends

friends

*"Faithless is he that says farewell when
the road darkens."*
— *J.R.R. Tolkien*

"There's no friends like the old friends."
— *James Joyce*

*"If you do not tell the truth about yourself,
you cannot tell it about other people."*
— *Virginia Woolf*

*"Each has his past shut in him like the
leaves of a book known to him by heart
and his friends can only read the title."*
— *Virginia Woolf*

*"Let us be grateful to the people who make us happy;
they are the charming gardeners
who make our souls blossom."*
— *Marcel Proust*

"Reading brings us unknown friends."
— *Honoré de Balzac*

*"I want to be with those who know
secret things or else alone."*
— *Rainer Maria Rilke*

*"If you live to be a hundred, I want to live to be
a hundred minus one day so I never have
to live without you."*
— *Joan Powers*

*"Books are the quietest and most constant of friends.
They are the most accessible and wisest of counselors,
and the most patient of teachers."*
— *Charles William Eliot*

"Friendship is a sheltering tree."
— *Samuel Taylor Coleridge*

*"Your friend is the man who knows all about you,
and still likes you."*
— *Elbert Hubbard*

*"The friendship that can come to an end,
never really began."*
— *Publilius Syrus*

"Those see nothing but faults that seek for nothing else."
— *Thomas Fuller*

*"No person is your friend who demands your silence,
or denies your right to grow."*
— Alice Walker

*"Don't walk in front of me...I may not follow
Don't walk behind me...I may not lead
Walk beside me...just be my friend."*
— Albert Camus

*"Words are easy, like the wind; faithful friends are
hard to find."*
— William Shakespeare

*"Friends show their love in times of trouble, not in
happiness."*
— Euripides

"The best mirror is an old friend."
— George Herbert

*"Animals are such agreeable friends — they ask no
questions, they pass no criticisms."*
— George Eliot

"Love is blind. Friendship closes its eyes."
— Friedrich Nietzsche

*"The friend who holds your hand and says the
wrong thing is made of dearer stuff than
the one who stays away."*
— *Barbara Kingsolver*

*"Our perfect companions never have fewer
than four feet."*
— *Sidonie Gabrielle Colette*

*"Each friend represents a world in us,
a world possibly not born until they arrive,
and it is only by this meeting that a new world is born."*
— *Anaïs Nin*

*"However rare true love may be, it is less so
than true friendship."*
— *Albert Einstein*

*"In prosperity our friends know us;
in adversity we know our friends."*
— *John Churton Collins*

"True friends are always together in spirit."
— *L.M. Montgomery*

"A friend to all is a friend to none."
— *Aristotle*

"I desire the things that will destroy me in the end."
— *Sylvia Plath*

*"There is no surer foundation for a beautiful friendship
than a mutual taste in literature."*
— *P.G. Wodehouse*

"What is a friend? A single soul dwelling in two bodies."
— *Aristotle*

*"I would rather walk with a friend in the dark,
than alone in the light."*
— *Helen Keller*

"Set your life on fire. Seek those who fan your flames."
— *Jalāl ad-Dīn Muhammad Balkhī Rumi*

*"Think where man's glory most begins,
and say my glory was I had such friends."*
— *William Butler Yeats*

*"Only a true best friend can protect you from
your immortal enemies."*
— *Richelle Mead*

life

life

*"Do no harm and leave the world a
better place than you found it."*
— *Patricia Cornwell*

"He was jealous of her future, and she of his past."
— *Anaïs Nin*

*"The price of anything is the amount of life
you exchange for it."*
— *Henry David Thoreau*

*"The hardest thing about the road not taken
is that you never know where it might have led."*
— *Lisa Wingate*

*"One day in the country
Is worth a month in town."*
— *Christina Rossetti*

*"Only those who will risk going too far
can possibly find out how far one can go."*
— *T.S. Eliot*

"Peace is always beautiful."
— *Walt Whitman*

"Always try to keep a patch of sky above your life."
— *Marcel Proust*

*"My destination is no longer a place, rather a
new way of seeing."*
— *Marcel Proust*

*"As soon as you trust yourself,
you will know how to live."*
— *Johann Wolfgang von Goethe*

*"Act as if what you do makes a difference.
It does."*
— *William James*

*"We've got to live, no matter how many
skies have fallen."*
— *D.H. Lawrence*

*"Growing up is losing some illusions,
in order to acquire others."*
— *Virginia Woolf*

"There is no greater sorrow
Than to recall a happy time
When miserable."
— *Dante Alighieri*

"We need never be ashamed of our tears."
— *Charles Dicken*

"What is life if not the shadow of a fleeting dream?"
— *Umberto Eco*

"My mistakes are my life."
— *Samuel Beckett*

"The only journey is the one within."
— *Rainer Maria Rilke*

"It is the lives we encounter that make life worth living."
— *Guy de Maupassant*

"Our greatest fears lie in anticipation."
— *Honoré de Balzac*

"The past beats inside me like a second heart."
— *John Banville*

*"There is no such thing as a great talent
without great willpower."*
— *Honoré de Balzac*

*"All that we see or seem is but
a dream within a dream."*
— *Edgar Allan Poe*

*"It takes courage to grow up and become
who you really are."*
— *e.e. cummings*

*"The world is full of magic things,
patiently waiting for our senses to grow sharper."*
— *William Butler Yeats*

*"I am no bird; and no net ensnares me:
I am a free human being with an independent will."*
— *Charlotte Brontë*

*"Oh, earth, you're too wonderful for
anybody to realize you."*
— *Thornton Wilder*

"The human soul needs beauty more than bread."
— *D.H. Lawrence*

"Life isn't about finding yourself.
Life is about creating yourself."
— *George Bernard Shaw*

"There comes a time in your life when
you have to choose to turn the page,
write another book or simply close it."
— *Shannon L. Alder*

"Hold to the now, the here, through which
all future plunges to the past."
— *James Joyce*

"All we have to decide is what to do
with the time that is given us."
— *J.R.R. Tolkien*

"You cannot find peace by avoiding life."
— *Michael Cunningham*

"Advice is what we ask for when we already know
the answer but wish we didn't."
— *Erica Jong*

"Your battles inspired me —
not the obvious material battles
but those that were fought and won
behind your forehead."
— *James Joyce*

"Even thou who mournst the daisies' fate,
that fate is thine."
— *Robert Burns*

"Life must go on; I forget just why."
— *Edna St. Vincent Millay*

"What a wonderful life I've had!
I only wish I'd realized it sooner."
— *Sidonie Gabrielle Colette*

"Of all human foibles love of living is the most powerful."
— *Jean-Baptiste Poquelin, Molière*

"Seek to please many, and you seek a failure."
— *Publilius Syrus*

"You can cut all the flowers but you cannot
keep Spring from coming."
— *Pablo Neruda*

*"Life is not measured by the number of breaths we take,
but by the moments that take our breath away."*
— *Maya Angelou*

"Life is half spent before we know what it is."
— *George Herbert*

*"We are born crying, live complaining,
and die disappointed."*
— *Thomas Fuller*

"I'm so glad I live in a world where there are Octobers."
— *L M. Montgomery*

*"Once in a while I am struck all over again...
by just how blue the sky appears...on wind-played
autumn mornings, blue enough to bruise a heart."*
— *Sanober Khan*

*"We are what we pretend to be, so we must be
careful about what we pretend to be."*
— *Kurt Vonnegut*

*"In three words I can sum up everything I've learned
about life: it goes on."*
— *Robert Frost*

"You will do foolish things but do them with enthusiasm!"
— *Sidonie Gabrielle Colette*

"Everything we shut our eyes to,
everything we run away from, everything we deny,
denigrate, or despise, serves to defeat us in the end."
— *Henry Miller*

"Life is a tragedy to those who feel and a comedy
to those who think."
— *Jean-Baptiste Poquelin, Molière*

"If you look for a meaning, you'll miss
everything that happens."
— *Andrei Tarkovsky*

"It's necessary to have wished for death in order
to know how good it is to live."
— *Alexandre Dumas*

"I was born lost and take no pleasure in being found."
— *John Steinbeck*

"Our own heart, and not other men's opinions,
forms our true honour."
— *Samuel Taylor Coleridge*

*"It was one of those March days when the sun shines
hot and the wind blows cold: when it is summer in
the light, and winter in the shade."*
— *Charles Dickens*

"To be alive at all is to have scars."
— John Steinbeck

*"It is more fitting for a man to laugh at life
than to lament over it."*
— Seneca

*"There is a saying that no man has tasted
the full flavour of life until he has known poverty,
love, and war."*
— O. Henry

"There is no wealth but life."
— John Ruskin

*"Right or wrong, it's very pleasant to break something
from time to time."*
— Fyodor Dostoevsky

*"Days follow days in flight, and every day is taking
Fragments of being, while together you and I
Make plans to live..."*
— Aleksandr Pushkin

*"Civilization will not attain to its perfection until the
last stone from the last church falls on the last priest."*
— Émile Zola

"Man's loneliness is but his fear of life."
— *Eugene O'Neill*

"The tragedy of life is not so much what men suffer,
but rather what they miss."
— *Thomas Carlyle*

"Where there's life there's hope."
— *J.R.R. Tolkien*

"Life, although it may only be an accumulation
of anguish, is dear to me, and I will defend it."
— *Mary Shelley*

"Summer will end soon enough, and childhood as well."
— *George R.R. Martin*

"There are two tragedies in life. One is to lose your
heart's desire. The other is to gain it."
— *George Bernard Shaw*

"War is what happens when language fails."
— *Margaret Atwood*

"Dreams are necessary to life."
— *Anaïs Nin*

"It is better to be hated for what you are than to be loved for what you are not."
— *André Gide*

"We delight in the beauty of the butterfly, but rarely admit the changes it has gone through to achieve that beauty."
— *Maya Angelou*

"Unbeing dead isn't being alive."
— *e.e. cummings*

"To know what life is worth you have to risk it once in a while."
— *Jean-Paul Sartre*

"Without music, life would be a mistake."
— *Friedrich Nietzsche*

"Life is a frail moth Caught in the web of years that pass..."
— *Sara Teasdale*

"The aim of life is to live, and to live means to be aware, joyously, drunkenly, serenely, divinely aware."
— *Henry Miller*

"Childhood is the kingdom where nobody dies.
Nobody that matters, that is."
— *Edna St. Vincent Millay*

"Order is the key to all problems."
— *Alexandre Dumas*

"A man's silence is wonderful to listen to."
— *Thomas Hardy*

"Let me live, love, and say it well in good sentences."
— *Sylvia Plath*

"Nothing ever becomes real until experienced."
— *John Keats*

"There is only one corner of the universe where you
can be certain of improving, and that's your own self."
— *Aldous Huxley*

"The insatiable thirst for everything which
lies beyond, and which life reveals, is the most
living proof of our immortality."
— *Charles Baudelaire*

"Life is ours to be spent, not to be saved."
— *D.H. Lawrence*

"Far away there in the sunshine are my highest aspirations. I may not reach them, but I can look up and see their beauty, believe in them, and try to follow where they lead."
— *Louisa May Alcott*

"My course is set for an uncharted sea."
— *Dante Alighieri*

"We all have our time machines, don't we? Those that take us back are memories... And those that carry us forward, are dreams."
— *H.G. Wells*

"Life is a journey that must be travelled no matter how bad the roads and accommodations."
— *Oliver Goldsmith*

"A man travels the world over in search of what he needs and returns home to find it."
—*George A. Moore*

"Circumstances are the rulers of the weak; they are but the instruments of the wise."
— *Samuel Lover*

"When we think of the past it's the beautiful things we pick out. We want to believe it was all like that."
— *Margaret Atwood*

"Difficulties are just things to overcome, after all."
— *Ernest Shackleton*

"Life itself is the most wonderful fairy tale."
— *Hans Christian Andersen*

loss

loss

*"It comes so soon, the moment when
there is nothing left to wait for."*
— *Marcel Proust*

*"What man of us has never felt,
walking through the twilight,
or writing down a date from his past,
that he has lost something infinite?"*
— *Jorge Luis Borges*

*"Tears shed for another person are not a
sign of weakness. They are a sign of a pure heart."*
— *José N. Harris*

*"Anyone who has lost something they thought
was theirs forever finally comes to realise
that nothing really belongs to them."*
— *Paulo Coelho*

*"In the English language there are
orphans and widows, but there is no word
for the parents who lose a child."*
— *Jodi Picoult*

"Never to suffer would never to have been blessed."
— *Edgar Allan Poe*

*"The fear of loss... it can destroy you as much
as the loss itself."*
— *Sarah J. Maas*

*"Remembering. Forgetting.
I'm not sure which is worse."*
— *Kelley Armstrong*

*"The whole world can become the enemy
when you lose what you love."*
— *Kristina McMorris*

*"Life is full of grief, to exactly the degree we allow
ourselves to love other people."*
— *Orson Scott Card*

"We all have an old knot in the heart we wish to untie."
— *Michael Ondaatje*

"Come back. Even as a shadow, even as a dream."
— *Euripides*

"Absence is a house so vast that inside
you will pass through its walls
and hang pictures on the air."
— Pablo Neruda

"If I can stop one heart from breaking,
I shall not live in vain."
— Emily Dickinson

"Often it feels like I am breathing today
only because a few years back
I had no idea which nerve to cut..."
— Sanhita Baruah

"It's not the endings that will haunt you
But the space where they should lie,
The things that simply faded
Without one final wave goodbye."
— Erin Hanson

"I am ashes where once I was fire..."
— George Gordon, Lord Byron

"Every loss is unprecedented."
— John Green

"There is no grief like the grief that does not speak."
— *Henry Wadsworth Longfellow*

"The fact that grief takes so long to resolve is not a sign of inadequacy but betokens depth of soul."
— Donald Woods Winnicott

"Lie still, lie still, my breaking heart;
My silent heart, lie still and break:
Life, and the world, and mine own self, are changed
For a dream's sake."
— Christina Rossetti

"I have a lot of work to do today;
I need to slaughter memory,
Turn my living soul to stone
Then teach myself to live again."
— Anna Akhmatova

"Don't grieve.
Anything you lose comes round in another form."
— Jalāl ad-Dīn Muhammad Balkhī Rumi

"When you have a sorrow that is too great it leaves no room for any other."
— Émile Zola

"Death always leaves one singer to mourn."
— Katherine Anne Porter

"To survive, you must tell stories."
— *Umberto Eco*

*"Sharing tales of those we've lost is how
we keep from really losing them."*
— Mitch Albom

*"I had someone once who made every day
mean something. And now.... I am lost....
And nothing means anything anymore."*
— Ranata Suzuki

*"It's so hard to forget pain, but it's even harder
to remember sweetness. We have no scar
to show for happiness. We learn so little from peace."*
— Chuck Palahniuk

*"Letting go means to come to the realization
that some people are a part of your history,
but not a part of your destiny."*
— Steve Maraboli

*"Loss alone is but the wounding of a heart;
it is memory that makes it our ruin."*
— Brian Ruckley

*"So I learned two things that night, and the next day,
from him: the perfection of a moment,
and the fleeting nature of it."*
— Margaret George

*"The broken heart. You think you will die,
but you just keep living, day after day after terrible day."*
— Charles Dickens

*"Let my thoughts come to you, when I am gone,
like the afterglow of sunset at the margin
of starry silence."*
— Rabindranath Tagore

*"Where are the songs I used to know,
Where are the notes I used to sing?
I have forgotten everything
I used to know so long ago."*
— Christina Rossetti

"Life begins on the other side of despair."
— Jean-Paul Sartre

*"To live is to suffer, to survive is to find
some meaning in the suffering."*
— Friedrich Nietzsche

*"It is often in the darkest skies that we
see the brightest stars."*
— Richard Evans

*"It's so much darker when a light goes out
than it would have been if it had never shone."*
— John Steinbeck

*"There is an ocean of silence between us…
and I am drowning in it."*
— Ranata Suzuki

"The past is never where you think you left it."
— Katherine Anne Porter

*"How could you go about choosing something
that would hold the half of your heart you had to bury?"*
— Jodi Picoult

*"We do not remember days,
we remember moments."*
— Cesare Pavese

"The wounds that never heal can only be mourned alone."
— James J. Frey

*"I have poured my heart out ….
And now I am empty."*
— Ranata Suzuki

*"Nothing is so painful to the human mind as a great
and sudden change."*
— *Mary Shelley*

*"We must leave our mark on life while we have it in
our power."*
— *Karen Blixen*

"Even the darkest night will end and the sun will rise."
— *Victor Hugo*

*"So many memories and so little worth remembering,
and in front of me, a long, long road
without a goal."*
— *Ivan Turgenev*

"It was my destiny to love and say goodbye."
— *Pablo Neruda*

"I have felt the wind of the wing of madness."
— *Charles Baudelaire*

"I am the immense shadow of my tears."
— *Federico Garcia Lorca*

*"Death walks faster than the wind and
never returns what he has taken."*
— Hans Christian Andersen

dreams

dreams

"You have to live where you wake up,
even if someone else dreamed you there."
— *Patricia Cornwell*

"There is only one thing that makes a dream
impossible to achieve: the fear of failure."
— *Paulo Coelho*

"I like the night. Without the dark,
we'd never see the stars."
— *Stephenie Meyer*

"Don't be pushed around by the fears in your mind.
Be led by the dreams in your heart."
— *Roy T. Bennet*

"I love those who yearn for the impossible."
— *Johann Wolfgang von Goethe*

"Worse than not realizing the dreams
of your youth would be to have been young
and never dreamed at all."
— *Jean Genet*

*"The future belongs to those who
believe in the beauty of their dreams."*
— *Eleanor Roosevelt*

"Dreams are the touchstones of our characters."
— *Henry David Thoreau*

*"I wish you to know that you have been
the last dream of my soul."*
— *Charles Dickens*

*"You're never given a dream without
also being given the power to make it true."*
— *Richard Bach*

*"It can take years to mould a dream.
It takes only a fraction of a second for it to be shattered."*
— *Mary E. Pearson*

"In dreams begin responsibilities."
— *William Butler Yeats*

"The mind was dreaming. The world was its dream."
— *Jorge Luis Borges*

"He who robs us of our dreams robs us of our life."
— *Virginia Woolf*

*"Sometimes we get through adversity
only by imagining what the world might be like
if our dreams should ever come true."*
— *Arthur Golden*

*"Reach high, for stars lie hidden in you.
Dream deep, for every dream precedes the goal."*
— *Rabindranath Tagore*

*"You see things; you say, 'Why?'
But I dream things that never were;
and I say, 'Why not?'"*
— *George Bernard Shaw*

"It does not do to dwell on dreams and forget to live."
— *J.K. Rowling*

*"When you compare the sorrows of real life to the
pleasures of the imaginary one, you will never
want to live again, only to dream forever."*
— *Alexandre Dumas*

*"Sometimes things become possible
if we want them bad enough."*
— T.S. Eliot

*"Hold fast to dreams,
For if dreams die
Life is a broken-winged bird,
That cannot fly."*
— Langston Hughes

*"Never did the world make a queen of a girl
who hides in houses and dreams without traveling."*
— Roman Payne

"In the eyes of mourning the land of dreams begins."
— Pablo Neruda

*"And the trouble is, if you don't risk anything,
you risk even more."*
— Erica Jong

"We are our choices."
— Jean-Paul Sartre

"The real world is much smaller than the imaginary."
— Friedrich Nietzsche

"The morning was full of sunlight and hope."
— *Kate Chopin*

"My dreams, my dreams! What has become of their sweetness? What indeed has become of my youth?"
— *Aleksandr Pushkin*

"Keep true to the dreams of thy youth."
— *Friedrich Schiller*

"The mystery of human existence lies not in just staying alive, but in finding something to live for."
— *Fyodor Dostoevsky*

"People see what they think is there."
— *Terry Pratchett*

"Beauty will save the world."
— *Fyodor Dostoevsky*

"We don't see things as they are, we see them as we are."
— *Anaïs Nin*

"The world of reality has its limits; the world of imagination is boundless."
— *Jean-Jacques Rousseau*

"There is nothing like a dream to create the future."
— Victor Hugo

"Perhaps when we find ourselves wanting everything,
it is because we are dangerously close
to wanting nothing."
— Sylvia Plath

"Sometimes the price of dreams is achieving them."
— Michael J. Sullivan

"The voice of the sea is seductive, never ceasing,
whispering, clamouring, murmuring,
inviting the soul to wander in abysses of solitude."
— Kate Chopin

*"The sea always filled her with longing,
though for what she was never sure."*
— *Cornelia Funk*

memories

memories

"Bricks without straw are more easily made
than imagination without memories."
— Edward Plunkett, Lord Dunsany

"A man sees in the world what he carries in his heart."
— Johann Wolfgang von Goethe

"And the moral of the story is that you don't
remember what happened. What you remember
becomes what happened."
— John Green

"It is far harder to kill a phantom than a reality."
— Virginia Woolf

"Memories vanish when we want to remember
but fix themselves permanently in the mind
when we want to forget."
— Emil Cioran

"Man's memory shapes
Its own Eden within."
— Jorge Luis Borges

*"Memories are dangerous things. You turn them over
and over, until you know every touch and corner,
but still you'll find an edge to cut you."*
— *Mark Lawrence*

*"Memories warm you up from the inside.
But they also tear you apart."*
— *Haruki Murakami*

"Sometimes, remembering hurts too much."
— *Jess Rothenberg*

"Memory is the diary we all carry about with us."
— *Oscar Wilde*

*"Love is a state in which a man sees things
most decidedly as they are not."*
— *Friedrich Nietzsche*

*"The only real treasure is in your head.
Memories are better than diamonds
and nobody can steal them from you."*
— *Rodman Philbrick*

"What are we, if not an accumulation of our memories?"
— *S.J. Watson*

*"It is easy to love people in memory;
the hard thing is to love them when they are
there in front of you."*
— *John Updike*

*"When it comes to memories,
the good and the bad never balance."*
— *Jodi Picoult*

*"It's regrets that make painful memories.
When I was crazy, I did everything just right."*
— *Mark Vonnegut*

*"Time, which changes people, does not alter the image
we have of them."*
— *Marcel Proust*

*"Scars have the strange power to remind us
that our past is real."*
— *Cormac McCarthy*

*"If I had a flower for every time I thought of you...
I could walk through my garden forever."*
— *Alfred, Lord Tennyson*

"Grey rocks, and greyer sea,
And surf along the shore --
And in my heart a name
My lips shall speak no more."
— *Charles G.D. Roberts*

"How we need another soul to cling to."
— *Sylvia Plath*

"Humans, not places, make memories."
— *Ama Ata Aidoo*

"The voice of the sea speaks to the soul."
— *Kate Chopin*

"Life cannot go on without a great deal of forgetting."
— *Honoré de Balzac*

freedom

freedom

*"As I would come to discover later in life, one shouldn't
be condemned for simply craving freedom."*
— Ira Wagler

"When I discover who I am, I'll be free."
— Ralph Ellison

*"You can have peace. Or you can have freedom.
Don't ever count on having both at once."*
— Robert A. Heinlein

"Anxiety is the dizziness of freedom."
— Søren Kierkegaard

*"Freeing yourself was one thing,
claiming ownership of that freed self was another."*
— Toni Morrison

*"The secret of happiness is freedom;
the secret of freedom is courage."*
— Carrie Jones

*"There's no freedom quite like the freedom
of being constantly underestimated."*
— Scott Lync

"She had not known the weight until she felt the freedom."
— Nathaniel Hawthorne

*"Take your life in your own hands, and what happens?
A terrible thing: no one to blame."*
— Erica Jong

*"There is a huge amount of freedom that
comes to you when you take nothing personally."*
— Don Miguel Ruiz

*"Freedom is not something that anybody
can be given. Freedom is something people take,
and people are as free as they want to be."*
— James Baldwin

*"Lock up your libraries if you like;
but there is no gate, no lock,
no bolt that you can set upon
the freedom of my mind."*
— Virginia Woolf

"Freedom lies in being bold."
— Robert Frost

"Freedom is what we do with what is done to us."
— Jean-Paul Sartre

"A friend is someone who gives you
total freedom to be yourself."
— Jim Morrison

"I don't argue with my enemies;
I explain to their children."
— André Malraux

"Travelers, there is no path,
paths are make for walking."
— Antonio Machado

"Never stand begging for that which you have
the power to earn."
— Miguel de Cervantes Saavedra

"Yesterday I dared to struggle,
today I dare to win."
— Bernadette Devlin

"Wild honey smells of freedom
The dust – of sunlight
The mouth of a young girl, like a violet
But gold – smells of nothing."
— Anna Akhmatova

happiness

happiness

"I built a fire and sat facing a window of darkness
where at sunrise I knew I would find the sea."
— Patricia Cornwell

"No medicine cures what happiness cannot."
— Gabriel García Márquez

"Man only likes to count his troubles;
he doesn't calculate his happiness."
— Fyodor Dostoevsky

"Happiness is beneficial for the body,
but it is grief that develops the powers of the mind."
— Marcel Proust

"Success is getting what you want,
happiness is wanting what you get."
— W. P. Kinsella

"Often, we pass beside happiness without seeing it,
without looking at it, or even if we have seen
and looked at it, without recognizing it."
— Alexandre Dumas

"Happiness is a gift and the trick is not to expect it,
but to delight in it when it comes."
— *Charles Dickens*

"Take responsibility of your own happiness,
never put it in other people's hands."
— *Roy T. Bennett*

"All happiness depends on courage and work."
— *Honoré de Balzac*

"Time you enjoy wasting is not wasted time."
— *Marthe Troly-Curtin*

"There are perhaps no days of our childhood we lived so
fully as those we spent with a favourite book."
— *Marcel Proust*

"I am not proud, but I am happy; and happiness blinds,
I think, more than pride."
— *Alexandre Dumas*

"It is spring again. The earth is like a child
that knows poems by heart."
— *Rainer Maria Rilke*

*"You will never be happy if you continue
to search for what happiness consists of.
You will never live if you are looking
for the meaning of life."*
— *Albert Camus*

"My heart is like a singing bird."
— *Christina Rossetti*

*"Summer has filled her veins with light
and her heart is washed with noon."*
— *C. Day Lewis*

"No man is happy unless he believes he is."
— *Publilius Syrus*

*"To sit with a dog on a hillside on a glorious
afternoon is to be back in Eden, where doing nothing
was not boring — it was peace."*
— *Milan Kundera*

"Children see magic because they look for it."
— *Christopher Moore*

"Unhappiness is the ultimate form of self-indulgence."
— *Tom Robbins*

"Happy is the people who need no heroes."
— Bertolt Brecht

*"Luxury is not a necessity to me, but beautiful
and good things are."*
— *Anaïs Nin*

"Total absence of humor renders life impossible."
— *Sidonie Gabrielle Colette*

*"We should read to give our souls
a chance to luxuriate."*
— *Henry Miller*

*"To put everything in balance is good,
to put everything in harmony is better."*
— *Victor Hugo*

*"The sweetest pleasure arises from
difficulties overcome."*
— *Publilius Syrus*

*"The pain of parting is nothing to the
joy of meeting again."*
— *Charles Dickens*

"The secret of joy is the mastery of pain."
— *Anaïs Nin*

"Why can't people have what they want?
The things were all there to content
everybody; yet everybody has the
wrong thing."
— *Ford Madox Ford*

"I'm not afraid of storms, for I'm
learning how to sail my ship."
— *Louisa May Alcott*

"There are many kinds of beauty as
there are habitual ways of seeking
happiness."
— *Charles Baudelaire*

"A little morphine in all the air. It
would be wonderfully refreshing
for everyone."
— *D.H. Lawrence*

"I've always imagined that Paradise
will be a kind of library."
— *Jorge Luis Borges*

"I have drunken deep of joy,
And I will taste no other wine tonight."
— *Percy Bysshe Shelley*

*"Just living is not enough," said the butterfly.
"One must have sunshine, freedom, and a little flower."
— Hans Christian Andersen*

books

books

*"All that I know about my life, it seems,
I have learned in books."*
— *Jean-Paul Sartre*

"Literature is my Utopia."
— *Helen Keller*

*"If you have a garden and a library,
you have everything you need."*
— *Cicero*

"A book must be the axe for the frozen sea within us."
— *Franz Kafka*

*"In the depth of winter, I finally learned that
there was in me an invincible summer."*
— *Albert Camus*

*"I write only because
There is a voice within me
That will not be still."*
— *Sylvia Plath*

"Above all things — read. Read the great stylists who cannot be copied rather than the successful writers who must not be copied."
— Ngaio Marsh

"To acquire the habit of reading is to construct for yourself a refuge from almost all the miseries of life."
— W. Somerset Maugham

"Man reading should be man intensely alive. The book should be a ball of light in one's hand."
— Ezra Pound

"To learn to read is to light a fire; every syllable that is spelled out is a spark."
— Victor Hugo

"And, moreover, to succeed, the artist must possess the courageous soul."
— Kate Chopin

"In the winter she curls up around a good book and dreams away the cold."
— Ben Aaronovitch

"The world was hers for the reading."
— Betty Smith

"People can lose their lives in libraries.
They ought to be warned."
— *Saul Bellow*

"Books are the plane, and the train, and the road.
They are the destination, and the journey.
They are home."
— *Anna Quindlen*

"Writing comes from reading, and reading is the finest
teacher of how to write."
— *Annie Proulx*

"I am too fond of reading books to care to write them."
— *Oscar Wilde*

"It is my ambition to say in ten sentences
what others say in a whole book."
— *Friedrich Nietzsche*

"A half-read book is a half-finished love affair."
— *David Mitchell*

"Some of these things are true and some of them lies.
But they are all good stories."
— *Hilary Mantel*

"Literature is the most agreeable way of ignoring life."
— *Fernando Pessoa*

"One glance at a book and you hear the voice of another person, perhaps someone dead for 1,000 years.
To read is to voyage through time."
— *Carl Sagan*

"Reading is my favourite occupation,
when I have leisure for it and books to read."
— *Anne Brontë*

"Most of what makes a book 'good' is that we are reading it at the right moment for us."
— *Alain de Botton*

"I read for pleasure and that is the moment
I learn the most."
— *Margaret Atwood*

"Collect books, even if you don't plan on reading them right away. Nothing is more important
than an unread library."
— *John Waters*

"Words are all we have."
— *Samuel Beckett*

*"Words dazzle and deceive because they are mimed by
the face. But black words on a white page
are the soul laid bare."*
— Guy de Maupassant

*"If a story is not about the hearer, he will not listen.
And here I make a rule – a great and interesting story
is about everyone or it will not last."*
— John Steinbeck

*"A book is a garden, an orchard, a
storehouse, a party, a company by the way,
a counsellor, a multitude of counsellors."*
— Charles Baudelaire

*"Let others pride themselves about
how many pages they have written; I'd rather
boast about the ones I've read."*
— Jorge Luis Borges

*"One day, you will be old enough to start reading
fairytales again."*
— C.S. Lewis

*"Her reputation for reading a great deal hung about her
like the cloudy envelope of a goddess in an epic."*
— Henry James

*"To know how much there is to know is the
beginning of learning to live."*
— Dorothy West

*"Of all that is written I love only what a man
has written in his own blood."*
— Friedrich Nietzsche

"My life is a reading list."
— John Irving

*"You must write, and read, as if your life
depended on it."*
— Adrienne Rich

*"If one cannot enjoy reading a book over and over again,
there is no use in reading it at all."*
— Oscar Wilde

*"How much sooner one tires of anything than of a book!
When I have a house of my own, I shall be miserable
if I have not an excellent library."*
— Jane Austen

*"You don't have to burn books to destroy a culture. Just
get people to stop reading them."*
— Ray Bradbury

*"Give me books, French wine, fruit,
fine weather and a little music played out of
doors by somebody I do not know."*
— John Keats

"Stories of imagination tend to upset those without one."
— Terry Pratchett

*"Some moments are nice, some are
nicer, some are even worth writing about."*
— Charles Bukowski

Gran's favourite quotes

Gran's favourite quotes

*"There is no such thing as bad publicity...
except your own obituary."*
— *Brendan Behan*

*"Complications, usually lead to more complications,
and if you continue to complicate things,
you might end up dead in the Hospital,
due to complications!"*
— *Sean Dunne*

*"Sorry is the fool who trades his soul for a Corvette.
Thinks he'll get the girl, but he'll
only get the mechanic."*
— *Eddie Vedder*

"The man who rows the boat seldom has time to rock it."
— *Bill Copeland*

*"Another belief of mine:
that everyone else my age is an adult,
whereas I am merely in disguise."*
— *Margaret Atwood*

"An early morning walk is a blessing for the whole day."
— *Henry David Thoreau*

*"I am sure that if the mothers of various
nations could meet, there would be
no more wars."*
— E.M. Forster

"Whatever satisfies the soul is truth."
— Walt Whitman

"Some people are so much sunshine to the square inch."
— Walt Whitman

"Enjoy when you can and endure when you must."
— Johann Wolfgang von Goethe

*"I was a great believer in hot buttered toast
at all hours of the day."*
— Frank O'Connor

*"Nothing thicker than a knife's blade
separates happiness from melancholy."*
— Virginia Woolf

*"Everybody who tells you how to act
has whiskey on their breath."*
— John Updike

*"Being Irish, he had an abiding sense of tragedy,
which sustained him through temporary periods of joy."
— William Butler Yeats*

"Life is the art of drawing without an eraser."
— *John Christian*

*"If you are patient in one moment of anger,
you will escape a hundred days of sorrow."*
— *Rainer Maria Rilke*

*"May the wind under your wings bear you
where the sun sails and the moon walks."*
— *J.R.R. Tolkien*

*"There's man all over for you,
blaming on his boots the faults of his feet."*
— *Samuel Beckett*

*"If we take care of the moments,
the years will take care of themselves."*
— *Maria Edgeworth*

*"Fiction was invented the day Jonah arrived home
and told his wife that he was three days late
because he had been swallowed by a whale."*
— *Gabriel García Márquez*

"Experience is a good school. But the fees are high."
— *Heinrich Heine*

*"No pessimist ever discovered the secrets of the stars,
or sailed to an uncharted land,
or opened a new heaven to the human spirit."*
— Helen Keller

*"The art of living is always to make a good thing
out of a bad thing."*
— E. F. Schumacher

"Man is a soldier and life must be fought."
— Robert Burns

"Hope is a talent like any other."
— Storm Jameson

"God will forgive me. It's his job."
— Heinrich Heine

*"Nobody who says 'I told you so' has ever been,
or will ever be, a hero."*
— Ursula K. LeGuin

"Before you let the sun in, mind he wipes his shoes."
— Dylan Thomas

"Anyone can hold the helm when the sea is calm."
— Publilius Syrus

*"To be Irish is to know that in the end
the world will break your heart."*
— Daniel Patrick Moynihan

"He who laughs last has not yet heard the bad news."
— Bertolt Brecht

*"All human wisdom is contained in these two
words — 'Wait and Hope'."*
— Alexandre Dumas

"No one asked you to be happy. Get to work."
— Sidonie Gabrielle Colette

*"There is nothing in the world so irresistibly
contagious as laughter and good humor."*
— Charles Dickens

*"Certain thoughts are prayers. There are moments
when, whatever be the attitude of the body,
the soul is on its knees."*
— Victor Hugo

*"There is no salvation in becoming adapted
to a world which is crazy."*
— Henry Miller

"The older I grow, the more I distrust the familiar doctrine that age brings wisdom."
— *H. L. Mencken*

"Music is love in search of a word."
— *Sidonie Gabrielle Colette*

"The tragedy of life is not so much what men suffer,
but rather what they miss."
— *Thomas Carlyle*

"Even if there were only two men left in the world and
both of them saints, they wouldn't be happy. One of them
would be bound to try and improve the other.
That is the nature of things."
— *Frank O'Connor*

"Man's loneliness is but his fear of life."
— *Eugene O'Neill*

"I have no money, no resources, no hopes.
I am the happiest man alive."
— *Henry Miller*

"It's not that the Irish are cynical. It's rather that
they have a wonderful lack of respect for
everything and everybody."
— *Brendan Behan*

"Birth was the death of him."
— *Samuel Beckett*

"If we wait for the moment when everything,
absolutely everything is ready,
we shall never begin."
— *Ivan Turgenev*

"In still moments by the sea, life seems
large-drawn and simple. It is there we
can see into ourselves."
— *Rolf Edberg*

"My turn shall also come:
I sense the spreading of a wing."
— *Osip Mandelstam*

"Our worst misfortunes never happen,
and most miseries lie in anticipation."
— *Honoré de Balzac*

"To gain what is worth having,
it may be necessary to lose everything else."
— *Bernadette Devlin*

"A rat in a maze is free to go anywhere,
as long as it stays inside the maze."
— *Margaret Atwood*

"Never laugh at live dragons."
— *J.R.R. Tolkien*

*"The odd thing about people who had many books
was how they always wanted more."*
— *Patricia A. McKillip*

*"I did not attend his funeral, but I sent a nice letter
saying I approved of it."*
— *Mark Twain*

*"It takes a great deal of bravery to stand up to our
enemies, but just as much to stand up to our friends."*
— *J.K. Rowling*

*"Success is not final; failure is not fatal:
it is the courage to continue that counts."*
— *Winston S. Churchill*

"Above all, be the heroine of your life, not the victim."
— *Nora Ephron*

*"Too much sanity may be madness and the maddest
of all, to see life as it is and not as it should be."*
— *Miguel de Cervantes Saavedra*

"Life is too short to stuff a mushroom."
— *Storm Jameson*

*"When one burns one's bridges, what a very nice
fire it makes."*
— Dylan Thomas

*"Facing it, always facing it, that's the way
to get through. Face it."*
— Joseph Conrad

*"The absence of vices adds so little to the
sum of one's virtues."*
— Antonio Machado

*"I know there is no straight road
No straight road in this world
Only a giant labyrinth
Of intersecting crossroads."*
— Federico Garcia Lorca

*"Coming back to where you started
is not the same as never leaving."*
— Terry Pratchett

*"One of the greatest tragedies in life is to lose
your own sense of self and accept the version of you
that is expected by everyone else."*
— K.L. Toth

*"Let us go forth, the tellers of tales,
and seize whatever prey the heart long for,
and have no fear. Everything exists, everything is true,
and the earth is only a little dust under our feet."*
— *William Butler Yeats*

"To be prepared is half the victory."
— *Miguel de Cervantes Saavedra*

*"We must be willing to let go of the life
we have planned, so as to have the life that is
waiting for us."*
— *E.M. Forster*

*"Always, however brutal an age may actually
have been, its style transmits its music only."*
— *André Malraux*

*"The trouble with having an open mind, of course, is that
people will insist on coming along and trying
to put things in it."*
— *Terry Pratchett*

*"Knowledge is knowing that a tomato is a fruit.
Wisdom is knowing not to put it in a fruit salad."*
— *Brian O'Driscoll*

*"Everyone has a story to tell. All you have to do
is write it. But it's not that easy."*
— *Frank McCourt*

*"Regret is mostly caused by not having
done anything."*
— *Charles Bukowski*

*"If trouble comes when you least expect it
then maybe the thing to do is to always expect it."*
— *Cormac McCarthy*

"Life shrinks or expands in proportion to one's courage."
— *Anaïs Nin*

"Don't let the bastards grind you down."
— *Margaret Atwood*

*"Our revenge will be the laughter
of our children."*
— *Bobby Sands*

NOTES

"Closed in a room, my imagination becomes the universe, and the rest of the world is missing out."
— *Criss Jami*

"What really knocks me out is a book that, when you're all done reading it, you wish the author that wrote it was a terrific friend of yours and you could call him up on the phone whenever you felt like it."
— *J.D. Salinger*

*"We thought we had such problems.
How were we to know we were happy?"*
— *Margaret Atwood*

A tribute
to our favourite contemporary poet

Social media platforms are so ephemeral, sometimes you read amazing words you want to share with everyone but there is unfortunately no 'permanent copy', no bound book to stash amazing tweets, so we wanted to share with you here some breathtaking tweeted poetry we love by John R. Hinton.

Mr. Hinton graciously granted us permission to republish four of our favourite poems of his.

---

i do not seek the road less traveled
i seek where there is no road at all
i want places where no foot has ever fallen
please understand, i am not speaking
of forest, plain or desert
i am talking about
your mind, your heart, your soul
i want all the undiscovered places
unfathomed

'i wish it would rain'
her soul, arid too long
i know no dance to break the clouds
if i did i would dance furiously
for her i'd risk appearing a fool
instead, i will weep for her
offering my tears as blessing and balm
my heart for her a raging storm
to flood her sated

i'm watching a candle burn
it seems i've known no other life
just here in this chair
darkness interrupted by
faint, flickering light
my only awareness
my gaze upon the flame
melting wax flows like tears
as if the candle bears great sorrow
and i've been called to attend the grief

your pain, my pain
in anguish might love be reborn
our emotional earth scorched by fire
dare we to once again bloom
might we claw through the debris
reaching again for the light we call love
dare we be so resilient
knowing the fire might come again
and with it your pain, my pain

Original poetry by John R. Hinton

"Sometimes, on difficult days or nights, seeing a tiny 'like' on a tweet to a friend, brings a smile... It's a sweet moment of connection, giving meaning to relationships developed here [on Twitter] that have become constant, a wonderful part of our lives."
— *Cadhla Logan*

Twitter
@Cadhla_L

*"Remember me, even if it's only in a corner
and secretly. Don't let me go."*
— *Carlos Ruiz Zafón*

*...with special
thanks to
Silence Possum
for her friendship,
support and
encouragement,
forever in my
heart...*

*with love,
Cadhla*

Never forget your true friends.